OLGA'S FRUMPY FOLDS

By
Olga
Schpitfeir

Cartoons by Jackie Urbanovic
Graphic illustrations by Elroy Balgaard
Schpitfeir Enterprises

Published and Distributed by: SCHPITFEIR ENTERPRISES

Direct all inquiries to: P.O. Box 1426

                                  Minnetonka, MN 55343

Library of Congress Catalog Card Number TX 579 784

International Standard Book Number: 0 9607330 0 0

First Printing   August 1980

Second Printing   December 1980

Third Printing   October 1982

Fourth Printing   August 1983

THANK YOU

I cannot totally list all the names; but to my frumpy friends and family, that after the initial jokes and put downs, you encouraged and contributed.

I must say a special Thank You to my parents for their love and encouragement, especially my father, Ben W. Meinhardt, for his financial assistance in earlier printings.

My special thanks to Frank J. Stangel for giving me his time, knowledge, wisdom and marketing ideas.

. . . A special thank you to you Lord.

For I know the plans that I have for you, declares the Lord, plans for welfare and not for calamity to give you a future and a hope.

Jeremiah 29:11

It is time to add some pizzazz to your dinner table! If you don't already own cloth napkins, it is time for a new discovery. There are beautiful and alive colored napkins available to you. They come in solids, plaids, and prints of all kinds and for all occasions.

When your breakfast, lunch or dinner guests step up to your table, instantly impress them with their own eyes, and do this with color.

Color is the clincher. It is found everywhere. If you are aware of its potential you can add some very wonderful effects to your table and your meal.

One interesting way to add that color, and has been around for a long time is your napkins. So here are some tips for those cloth napkins.

Beginning with color, choose napkins with colors which relate directly to food; they are the most appetizing. Reds, oranges, greens, shades of brown and rich creams are the ones to seek.

Next, be aware of the fiber content, very important. Choose a napkin with absorbent qualities. Cotton and linen are good. You will also find synthetic fabrics. Try to choose a blend and not a napkin that is coated with sizing or bleach. Remember, you do wash them and once you do you will still want some body left.

Now comes the weave. There are several options. The point to remember is that the weave is going to have an important effect on the fold you choose and how you care for it. If you seriously dislike laundry, a coarse woven napkin may be the answer. It will add new depth and texture to the table, but if you enjoy folding napkins, it will be rather limiting. There are some where it looks dynamite.

A small weave will be more versatile for folding, but you need to be careful here too. A smaller woven napkin may be too soft and thin and will be unable to hold a good crease. Most of the folds in the book require or will look their best if they can be slightly stiff, and this will come through laundry care.

When you wash your napkins, I have found that if you put them in a dryer, they may turn out too limp and require light pressing. If you let them dry outside of the dryer, pressing may not be necessary. Once clean, remember to store them flat. Attention to detail is important. A well presented napkin will enhance a place setting; a poorly finished one will create a bad first impression on a guest.

Now for the fun part. When you look at the folds, do not be put off by the complicated appearance of some of the folds illustrated. They are presented in a logical manner that has been tested by male and female, so that the directions are readable and understandable.

All the folds have been done with square napkins, but the sizes may vary. Occasionally you will see an asterisk(*) by the illustration. That means that fold may be done using a napkin with a print only on one side.

Before beginning a new fold, read all of the directions thoroughly. The dotted lines in the illustrations signify the area of the napkin that is to be folded and the solid lines illustrate the napkin edge.

It is also important to place the napkin in the same position as the illustration and fold it in the same direction.

All the directions and illustrations have been carefully planned so that anyone will have success at their first attempt.

Remember:
   Creativity is the word.
   Napkins do not have to match.
   Mix colors and prints with tablecloths and placemats.
   Tuck a fresh flower into the napkin at the table.
   Look around the house for unusual napkin rings, lace, handles of
      cups and mugs, and even cookie cutters.
   Paper napkins may be substituted.
   And just because one fold may be under one section, be creative
      and think of some different ideas.

CONTENTS

STAND-UP INDEX

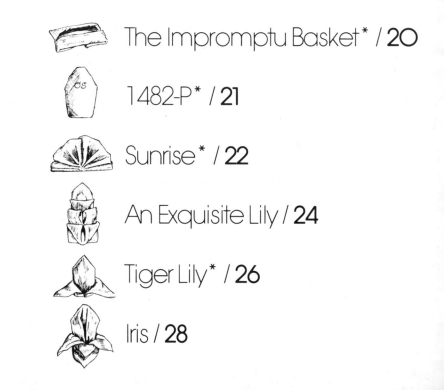
*A napkin printed only on
one side may be used.

8

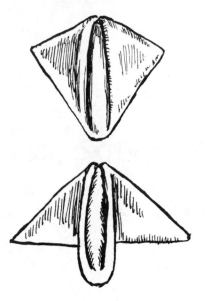

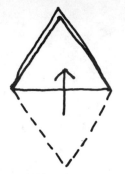

1. Flip the bottom up to form a triangle.

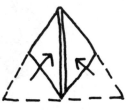

2. Flip the left and right corners toward the center, forming another diamond.

Flip over left to right, smooth side up.

3. Flip the bottom half up.

4. Take the starred corners and fold the napkin in half, folding the edges underneath.

The napkin naturally stands up.

To set your table, place the center edge point toward the chair.

Where it all began.

This napkin is extremely practical because many can be prefolded and stored for future use.

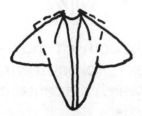

5. A little different look—
When the napkin is
standing up, take the
two back sections and
bring them forward.

A ruby is not lovelier than a rock,
an angel not more glorious than a frog.

11

THE BIRD
OF PARADISE

thank you Ray Duffy.

1. Fold in half and in half again.

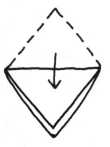

2. Fold in half, keeping all of the loose points together.

Now place in such a position that all of the loose points are on top.

3. Take both left and right points, folding them towards the center and lay flat.

4. Fold the upper extended

5. portions underneath, so
   one can't see it.

7. half; with the other, lift
   the petals up one by one
   and shape the bird.

6. With one hand fold in

If I am rehearsing it, isn't it
obvious that I want to do it?

OLGA'S
FAVORITE *

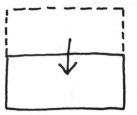

1. Fold the napkin in half.

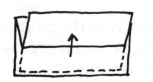

2. Fold the top layer in half again, but this time towards the initial center fold.

3. Do likewise with the other side.

4. End view.

It is tricky at first, but dynamite.

thank you Geraldine Halvston.

14

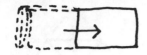

5. Fold in half the other way.

Turn the napkin so the loose edges are on top.

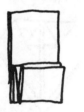

6. Take the top half of the napkin and fold in thirds (accordion style) towards the center fold.

Flip over and do likewise.

7. Important step: Grasp

8. the end side that has the raw napkin edges, grasping at the lowest edge. Take each * point and make a deep fold away from the original.

9. Turn it around in your hand. Take the adjacent * points and fold them away from the original position.

10. Squish together and fold each side panel down to finish off the pattern. Do on each side.

Grasp each end panel you just folded and fan out onto the table.

BISHOP'S HAT*

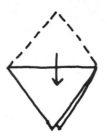

1. Fold the flat square napkin into a triangle.

2. Fold the right and left points to the center.

3. Fold the top corner down to one inch of the bottom point.

4. Turn the folded point back up to the upper edge.

Flip the napkin over, left to right and turn around 180 degrees (point the triangle up).

5. Fold the right and left points across and overlap, tucking one inside the other.

6. Stand the napkin up.

7. A variation that changes

8. the total look is to take the two loose corners and bring them down forming petals.

"ROLL" HER UP*

Use this fold for warm rolls, party favors or small gifts.

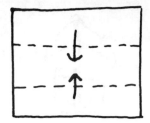

1. Put your napkin flat on the table and fold it exactly in three parts.

2. End View.

3. Fold both the left and right corners down along the dotted line shown.

4. Now turn up the bottom

5. edges, so you have a smooth lower edge.

6. Bring the left and right sides together inserting one into the other.

Stand up.

7. Fold the extra fabric down inside; you now have a cylinder with a bottom.

It's this simple: If I never try anything, I never learn anything. If I never take a risk, I stay where I am.

THE IMPROMPTU BASKET*

So simple you will not believe it. Its uses are varied; if you do not have a basket, use this one for your breads and crackers, for individuals or for large groups.

thank you Ray Duffy.

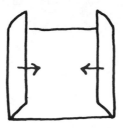

Depending on what size you need . . .

1. Roll each side to the center, the distance determining the basket size.

2. Flip over.

3. Take each end and fold towards the center.

Flip over again.

Open it up by working with the rolled edges. Set it on a plate, so you can pass it around.

1482-P*

If you have a design in one corner of your napkin and wish to show it off, even more . . .

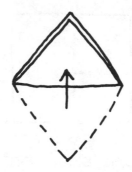

1. Flip the bottom up to form a triangle.

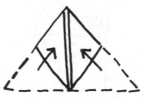

2. Flip the left and right corners toward the center, forming a diamond.

3. Flip the bottom point up and you form another triangle.

Now depending where your design is, you may have to flip it over.

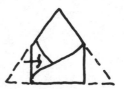

4. Now tuck one corner inside the other, forming a cylinder.

Stand up.

SUNRISE *

thank you Jody Earles.

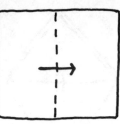

1. Beginning with a square napkin, fold it in half along the dotted line.

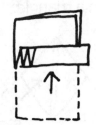

2. Start folding like an accordion. Fan fold up to one-fourth from the bottom making each fold two inches wide.

Flip over left to right.

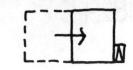

3. Fold in half.

4. Make sure the fanned edges are on the outside.

5. Grasp all of the top right corners into the fan folds, creating a diagonal fold.

6. Tip the napkin on the fold end and fan out the pleats.

He has not lived in vain who learns to be unruffled by loss, by gain, by joy, by pain.

AN EXQUISITE LILY

thanks for the help Mutley.

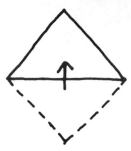

1. Fold the flat napkin to form a triangle.

2. Bring the left and right points up to the center, creating a diamond.

3. Bring the bottom point up using about two-thirds of the bottom half.

4. Fold back the tip, so it is even with the bottom edge.

5. Presently you have two free flaps; bring each of them down and tuck underneath the bottom point you just created from the previous step.

One more tuck —

6. Take the top point, that is loose (*), and tuck that underneath forming a third tier.

Flip over left to right, so smooth side is up.

7. Fold the right and left points across each other, tucking one inside the other.

8. Turn it around, stand it up and fluff out the sections.

What a lily.

PERSONAL POINTS

TIGER LILY *

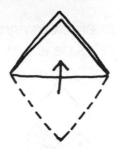

1. Flip the bottom up to form a triangle.

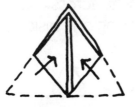

2. Flip the left and right corners toward the center, forming a diamond.

   Flip over left to right.

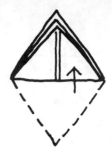

3. Flip the bottom half up.

4. Take the left and right corners, tuck one inside the other forming somewhat of a cylinder.

5. Turn it around and stand it up; bring each petal down.

Love is uncovered; it is carefully unveiled, like folding back petals.

IRIS

You need a good stiff napkin for this one.

1. Fold the bottom point towards the top, leaving a two inch difference.

2. Grasping both left and right corners, fold them towards the center, shaping the napkin into a diamond.

3. Take the bottom point and flip up forming a triangle.

   Now you have a smooth triangle.

4. Take the right and left corners, tuck the left corner into the right corner (enough so that it stays) forming a cylinder.

Grasp the napkin with the thumb in the center of the cylinder and the fingers on the outside.

Flip over left to right.

5. With the free hand, pull down the front flap and the remaining petals.

Stand it up.

The finest qualities of our nature, like the bloom on fruit, can be preserved only by the most delicate handling.
Henry David Thoreau

LILY
AT A BUD

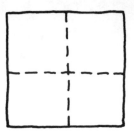

1. Lay your square napkin flat on the table and fold in half and in half again, ending in a smaller square.

2. Take the top layer turning the edge in and roll it half the way down.

3. It should look like this.

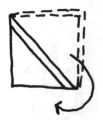

4. Take the remaining three loose corners, and fold them underneath, resulting in a triangular shape.

Flip over left to right.

5. Take the left and right
   corners, tuck one inside
   each other, forming a
   cylinder.

6. Stand up.

Hesitate and wait and wait or enter by another door.
The rules of man are made for breaking, but be sure
none has gone before.

THE CARDINALS CAP*

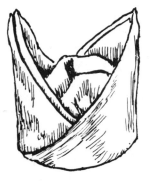

It is tricky, but go for it.

Fold your napkin in half with the open edges on top.

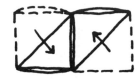

1. Fold the top left corner down and the bottom right corner up.

   Flip it over left to right

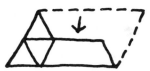

2. Fold the top half downward leaving the small triangle at left.

3. Reach over and find the hidden triangle and bring down.

4. Fold the left triangle in half.

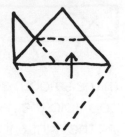

5. Fold up the lower triangle.

Flip over left to right.

6. Fold the left triangle in half and tuck the left corner into the right pocket.

Stand up.

LIL' BOOT*

Have you ever thought of having a special fold for a baby shower?

You need a starched napkin, **not** a soft one; even paper will work well.

thanks for the help Ben.

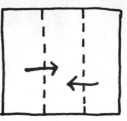

1. Fold the square napkin in thirds.

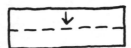

2. Now fold it in half lengthwise.

3. End view.

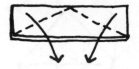

4. With the smooth edge on top, fold the napkin along the right and left dotted lines.

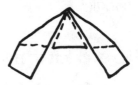

5. Now fold it again along the dotted line.

6. It should look like this.

7. Now, fold in half left to right, so the napkin looks like the illustration.

8. Holding the tip with your left hand, take the top extension and turn inside and up.

9. Take the second extension and fold in half.

10. Fold that extension in half and tuck into the tip of the shoe, creating a compact package.

11. Take the top extension and fold it inside out to form a cuff around the boot.

"OVER STARCHED" CUFF *

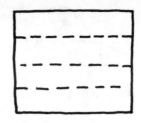

1. Fold the napkin in fourths.

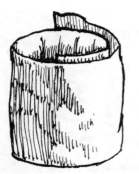

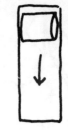

2. End View.

3. Take a round glass and place on napkin. Roll the napkin tightly around the glass and slip the glass out, not squishing the round form. Set the napkin up and place on the table.

4.

This one is extremely simple but it just might be Mr. Right.

"If something doesn't go well, it's because I haven't understood the composer." Toscanini

x

37

MEIN HUT*

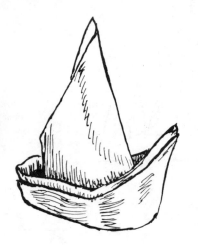

Need a hat for a birthday, a dunce or a sombrero?

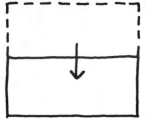

1. Fold the top half down.

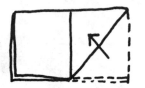

2. Take the far right corner and bring it up.

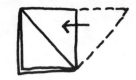

3. Do it again.

4. Now there is a square shape. Bring the right triangle down to form a triangle.

5. Grasp all of the open edges and look for the position that there is a clear funnel to the tip.

6. Now flip those edges and form a cuff around the entire cap.

Shape and stand up.

Surely this must be an ancient proverb:
If the situation is killing you, get out!

BABES

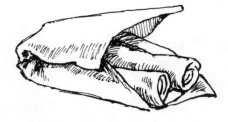

thanks Carolyn and Jerry

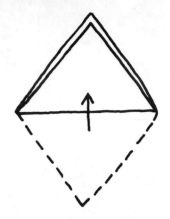

1. Fold the square napkin into a triangle.

2. Begin rolling each side towards the center.

3. Finished Look.

4. Fold it in half with the rolled edges in the center.

5. Take the top loose layer and fold it all the way back, so there is a loose flap on each side.

6. Babies all tucked in?

I wish my fold fit in here as well as a 1976 Pouilly Fuisse.

OLGA'S NEW LOVE

If this is your first time . . . read the directions <u>carefully</u> and <u>go slowly</u>.

1. Make two accordion pleats, dividing the napkin into thirds.

2. End view.

3. Fold the napkin in half, lengthwise. Observe the end view.

4. Make two accordion pleats. Observe diagram.

5. End view.

6. Fold the top flaps into triangles and press hard to crease.

Starting with the left, pick up the * point again and fold over to the right.

What you are doing is making triangles with each flap by reversing the crease in the middle of each pleat.

Do likewise with the right side

7. It will look like this; take the * point again and fold over to the right.

Do you not know that every failure brings with it the bud of an equivalent success.

CAMPERS *

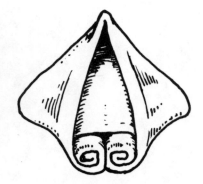

1. Fold your napkin lengthwise into four parts. Place the napkin so that the folded edge is on top.

2. End view.

3. Fold both the left and right corners down along the dotted line shown.

4. Flip over left to right.

5. Roll each extended section tightly up to the bottom of the triangle.

6. Bring the rolls to the center so that they are parallel with each other.

7. Flip over left to right. It will automatically shape itself. You may have to pull up on the point of the triangle to make it stand up.

"Go where others dare not go; down paths revealed in dreams. Chase shadows through the shadows; until you reach the sun."

VIVA*

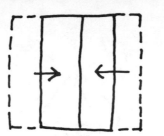

1. With the napkin lying flat, fold the outer edges toward the center line, making equal sections.

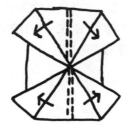

2. Place a finger in the center and fold out the four corners diagonally.

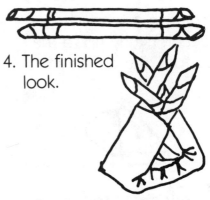

3. Roll tightly, each side to the center.

4. The finished look.

5. Bend up the ends, dividing the napkin into thirds. Interlock the alternating ends of the rolls to balance the fold.

BETHANY

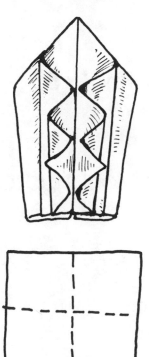

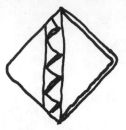

2. Arrange the napkin so that all loose points are to the right.

   Fold back the first layer — all the way to the center and accordion fold it.

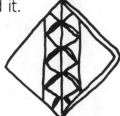

3. Take the second layer and do likewise; see diagram for the finished look.

Flip over left to right.

4. Bring the bottom point up using about two-thirds of the bottom half.

5. Fold the right and left points across each other, tucking one inside the other.

1. Fold the napkin in half and in half again.

GLASS STUFFERS INDEX

Candlestick* / **50**

Peacock Fan* / **55**

Combo-Candlestick Fan / **52**

Marnie's Mockingbird* / **56**

Fleur-De-Lys / **54**

Echoes* / **58**

*A napkin printed only on
one side may be used.

48

CANDLESTICK*

Use this as a centerpiece too. Fold three or five and set together using napkin rings on the bottom for stands, and decorate with dried flowers.

1. Take a flat napkin and fold it in half forming a triangle.

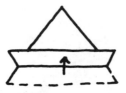

2. Next fold a hem along the folded edge, about one and one-half inches wide.

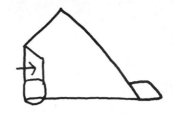

3. Flip over left to right. Begin at one end and roll to the other end.

4. Leave one inch unrolled; take that and stuff it into the hem.

SALUTE!

COMBO-CANDLESTICK FAN

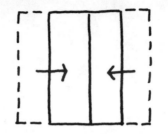

1. With the napkin laying flat, fold the outer edges toward the center line.

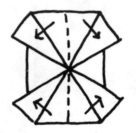

2. Fold out the four corners diagonally.

3. The top half: Roll very tightly to the center point; the bottom half: continue from the rolled and now accordion fold to the bottom.

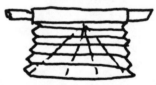

4. Fold in half with the candlesticks in the center and stuff into a goblet, fanning out the pleated portion.

"Blessed are the arts which do not require interpreters."

Botto

FLEUR-DE-LYS

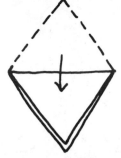

or:

A stylized three-petaled representation of an Iris flower.

1. Fold the napkin in half to form a triangle.

2. Two Options

    *Either fold the two tips up on one side or

    *Split the tips and fold them one on each side.

3. For both, accordion fold from one side to the other.

It is now ready to be stuffed in a glass and fluffed out.

If you choose option 2, a variation for that would be to bring the front point down over the glass and arrange like a waterfall.

PEACOCK FAN *

It is a variation from the fan fold, found in the napkin ring section.

1. Fold your square napkin so the end view looks like the illustration.

2. Accordion fold left to right the entire napkin.

3. Stuff one end in the glass and fan out. This one would work also with a napkin ring.

MARNIE'S MOCKING-BIRD *

This bird works well with a coarse woven napkin.

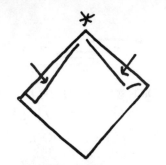

1. Holding the *corner tightly, begin rolling one side and then the other, or hold that * corner under your chin and roll each side at the same time.

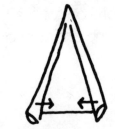

2. Finished look.

3. Now set in a wine goblet and shape into a bird, inserting the beak on the inside of the glass.

ECHOES*

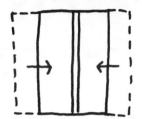

1. Bring the two sides together, to the middle.

2. Fold in half.

3. The end view.

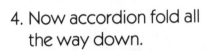

4. Now accordion fold all the way down.

5. Stuff the napkin in the glass making sure you set the single folded edge in the glass. Work with it and fan out to your taste.

KINA

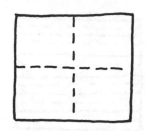

1. Fold your square napkin in half and in half again, creating a small square.

2. Fold your new square in half, creating a triangle.

3. It does not matter what side is up, but begin to accordion fold from one side to the other. Each one of these folds should be about one inch wide.

4. It will look something like this, from the side view.

Now hold the bottom and open out the pleats and arrange in your favorite glass.

FIRST EDITIONS*

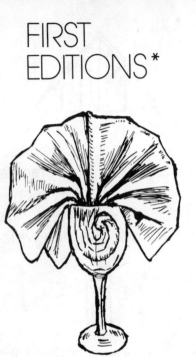

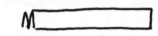

1. Take the flat napkin and

2. accordion fold pleats one inch wide all the way down.

3. Fold the napkin in half, roll the bottom edge so it will fit the wine glass, and stuff it in, then let go.

IT IS AS SIMPLE AS OLGA SAYS

1. Placing the flat napkin on a flat surface, with two fingers, pinch the napkin in the center and grab.

Stuff it into a wine goblet.

This fold is simple and may be used for individual placesettings and also as a centerpiece. If you use it as a centerpiece, get two candles and place them on either side.

Remember: You should have a point of interest on the table top. You shouldn't have too many things to look at. If you choose this centerpiece, use one of the jejune folds for your individual place setting, avoid the eye catching stand-up and glass stuffers.

It could be rabbit ears but I found it in

MAZATLAN.*

This looks dynamite with many at a table.

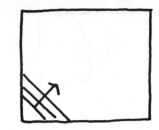

1. Take the square napkin and begin at the corner rolling it all the way to the opposite corner.

2. Fold it in half and set in a wine glass.

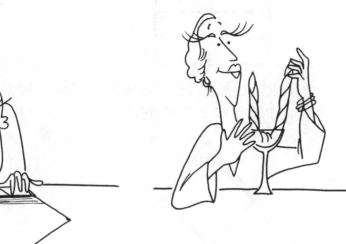

Whether it is writing a book, painting a picture or arranging a room, I do not believe that a person can do it his way without being creative.

PEONY

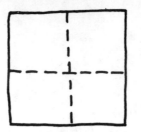

1. Fold your square napkin in half and in half again.

2. Keep all of the loose points on top.

3. Fold the bottom point up three inches.

4. Fold the napkin in half, vertically.

5. Accordion fold each half to the center; separately.

7. Tuck in the corners of each layer, into the fold, to form your Peony.

6. "Stuff" in your glass and separate the layers.

NAPKIN RING INDEX

 Fan* / **68**

 ''Wacco'' Tie* / **71**

 Olga's Second Simple Fold* / **69**

 Daisy* / **72**

Twin Cattails* / **70**

Bollo* / **74**

*A napkin printed only on one side may be used.

FAN*

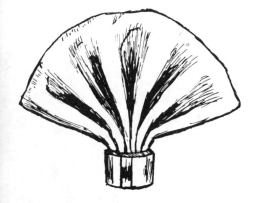

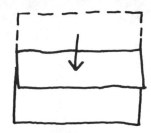

1. Lay napkin flat and turn down one-third from the top.

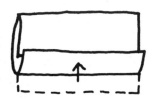

2. Bring the lower edge up one and one-half inches, overlap.

Turn vertically.

3. Make one inch pleats, accordion style, one end to the other.

4. With the smooth side facing you, stand up in a napkin ring.

thank you Mary Clark

OLGA'S SECOND SIMPLE FOLD*

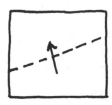

1. Lay napkin flat and fold it in half, but off center.

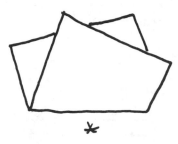

2. Then at * bring in both sides to the center and "ring it" with your favorite ring.

Look for some interesting napkin rings around your home.

*How about using your coffee cup or mug handle.

*Or an old spring and paint it up.

*Sew some lace or ribbon together.

*An old ring.

*Cookie cutters.

TWIN CATTAILS *

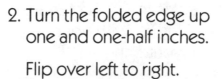

This is a variation from the candlestick.

thank you Mary Clark.

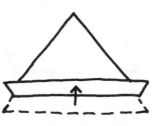

1. Fold your napkin into a large triangle.

2. Turn the folded edge up one and one-half inches.

   Flip over left to right.

3. Roll the left point to the center.

   Roll the right point to the center.

4. Making sure your base is even, hold firmly and stand in a napkin ring.

"WACCO" TIE *

thank you Mary Clark.

1. Turn up into a triangle.

2. Fold center point down two inches and roll until it becomes a strip.

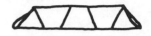

3. Fold in half.

Bring the points together and draw thru the napkin ring, forming the tie.

DAISY*

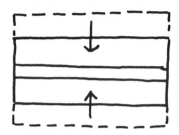

3. an accordion fashion, left end to right end, all the way down. Each fold should be roughly one and one-half inches wide.

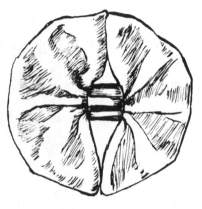

Instead of using a napkin ring, tie it together with lace.

1. Beginning with the square napkin, fold the top and bottom towards the center, leaving one inch of the center uncovered.

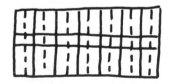

2. Next fold the napkin in

4. Slide a napkin ring down through the folds and to the center. Fan out the top and bottom to form the Daisy.

Instead of a napkin ring, clip the center with a decorative clip or name card, and then you are ready to fan it out.

The meaning of life is to see.

BOLLO *

It is a compact way to carry your flatware.

This is somewhat ad lib; it will be described from a napkin with one printed side.

1. Begin with the patterned side underneath; flip that bottom point up so a portion of the print is showing.
   Flip over left to right.

2. Bring bottom section up. Do not completely expose the full point. Flip over left to right.

3. Roll the left point and the right point, meeting in the center.

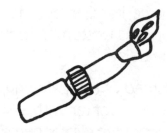

4. Slide the napkin ring on so it is contained; slide it past the hem. Now tie a knot at the top for interest.

FIVE POINT
FLUSH

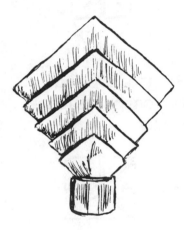

thank you Mary Clark.

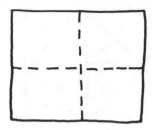

1. Fold in half and in half again.

2. With the open points at the bottom, bring the first corner one inch from the top point.

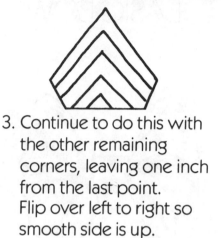

3. Continue to do this with the other remaining corners, leaving one inch from the last point. Flip over left to right so smooth side is up.

4. Fold the left point to the center and fold the right point to the center. Flip over and stand up in a napkin ring.

75

BASIC BOW *

thank you Mary Clark.

1. Beginning with your flat napkin, bring all four corners to the center. Crease.

2. Bring left and right corners to the center again.
Flip over left to right, so the smooth side is up.

3. Bring the top and bottom points to the center.

4. Keeping the points together, pinch the sides from the left and right.

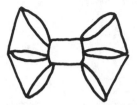

5. Slip the napkin ring over one side and work into the bow.

YOU'LL BE AMAZED WHERE YOU FIND FOLDS.

ROSE *

You will need a tall three inch napkin holder for this one.

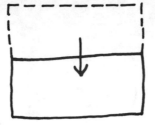

1. Fold the napkin in half, keeping the folded edge on top.

2. Starting at one end, begin to roll it tight until you have a solid center core, using about two inches of fabric.

3. Holding the center tightly . . . Gradually wrap the remainder of the fabric loosely around the center, pinching it with your fingers as you go.

When you have completed this . . . fold the extra fabric in half, that is hanging down.

Tuck the fold into a tall napkin ring. Work with it and shape it into . . .

A rose.

CASSANDRA *

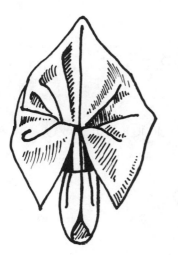

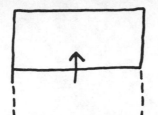

1. Fold the napkin in half with the open edges on top.

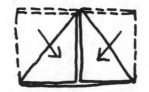

2. Fold the left and right point <u>down</u> to the center.

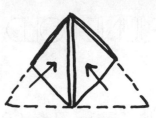

3. Now bring the left and right points <u>up</u> to the center.

Pinch the bottom point and sides together, then "ring it."

4. Peel back the top layer on each side.

JEJUNE FOLD INDEX

***A napkin printed only on
one side may be used.**

TRIPLE TIER

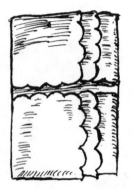

If you want to show off your edges — check this one out.

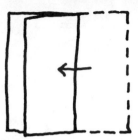

1. Fold the right edge over and leave two inches uncovered.

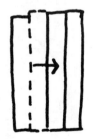

2. Back fold the flap and leave one inch uncovered.

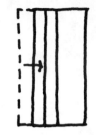

3. Take the left flap and fold over, leaving one inch.

4. End view.

Flip over left to right.

5. Fold the bottom up and the top down.

Friends eventually forgive and come back together because people need people more than they need pride.

THE CLASSIC: *

Never old, yet never new.

A fine delicate show off for scalloped edges.

1. Fold your napkin in half and in half again.

2. Fold the scalloped edges to the center point.

Flip over left to right and rotate the point to the bottom.

3. Bring the left and right corners to the center.

4. Flip over left to right and place on the plate.

PACE *

Personalize your Pace with a
place card or a flower.

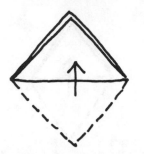

1. Fold the square napkin in
   half to form a triangle.

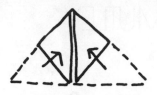

3. Now fold the two
   extended parts toward
   the center and form a
   square.

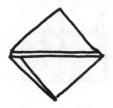

2. Fold in half again to form
   another triangle.

4. It is ready for the plate.

MUTLEY*

Very similar to Dudley but a
noticeable difference.

1. Fold your napkin in half
forming a triangle.

2. Fold the left and right
corners up, forming a
diamond.

3. Fold up half of the
bottom toward the top.

4. Fold that back down in
half.

5. Fold the left and right sides underneath.

6. Ready.

Am I a body or am I a mind riding a horse named body?

DUDLEY

1. Flip only half of the lower triangle up.

3. Fold half of the bottom up.

Very similar to Mutley but a noticeable difference.

This works better with a smaller napkin.

2. Fold the left and the right sides toward the center, finishing off a triangle.

4. Fold that tip down.

5. Fold the sides
   underneath to the width
   desired.

Play to the audience you know; they will respond to
you. But what's good to you is not to some. They just
never understand.

DOUBLE DIAGONAL

A perfect buffet fold.

thank you Jewel.

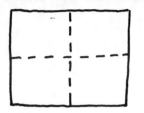

1. Fold in half and in half again.

2. Turn down the top free corner two inches and repeat twice.

3. Take the next free corner, turn down in the same manner until it is parallel to the previous fold.

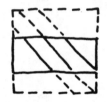

4. Fold under the top and bottom of the napkin.

Give the folded napkin a quarter of a turn twist, and place on your plate.

ZADA *

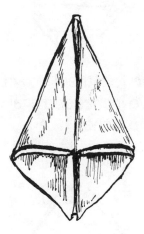

This is great with a coarsely woven napkin.

1. Fold the square napkin in half to form a triangle.

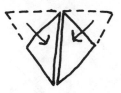

2. Bring the points down to form a square.

3. Bring the side points

4. down and form another odd shaped rectangle.

SILVER
STUFFERS

Ideal for buffets.

1. Fold the napkin in half and in half again.

2. Take the top two layers

3. and fold them down two inches and again two inches.
Flip over left to right.

4. Then fold the other two flaps two inches underneath.

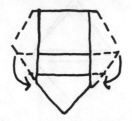

5. Fold the left and right points to the center.

6. Flip left to right to finish.

An honest person does not find himself in agreement with every enumerated belief held by the group of which he is a member.

BURWELL

OLGA

*Tuck flatware in

*Place name tags in between

*enjoy as is.

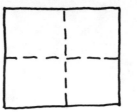

1. Fold in half and in half again.

2. Take the top flap and roll it to the center.

3. Take the second flap, and do likewise.

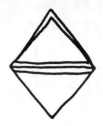

4. Now tilt the napkin so the folds are horizontal.

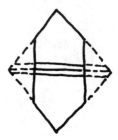

5. Now fold underneath each side.

The perfect man uses his mind as a mirror. It grasps nothing, it rejects nothing, it receives but does not keep.

ARTICHOKE *

Use individually for escargot or soup bowl liners. How about as a presentation for a small gift or a basket liner, or stuff it in a glass.

1. Starting off with a square napkin, fold each corner in to form a square.

2. Fold each of the newly made corners into the center again.
Flip over left to right so smooth square is available for the next step.

3. Fold the corners toward the center as you have done before.

Use a glass or your thumb and place it in the center so the top points do not pull loose.

4. Pull each of the points underneath, gently away and out.

5. Pull out all four points.

6. Between each point, go underneath and pull out the hidden bottom point.

Now place on a plate and begin.

PERSONAL POINTS

FOLLIES *

1. Starting off with a square napkin, fold each corner in to form a square.

2. Fold each of the newly made corners into the center again.

3. Do that again.

   Flip over left to right so smooth square is available for the next step.

4. Fold the corners toward the center as you have done before.

Where the artichoke has 8 points, Follies has 12.

5. Pull each of the points underneath, gently away and out.

6. Pull out all four points.

7. Between each point, go underneath and pull out the hidden bottom points.

8. Keep looking . . . There are four more points to find and pull out.

LA FRENCH FOLD*

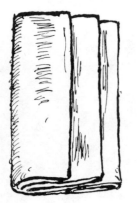

Simple but elegant.

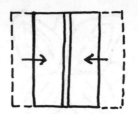

1. Fold each side in to meet at the center.

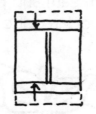

2. Fold each end side down.

Turn so it is going in the direction of the napkin illustrated.

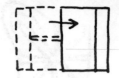

3. Fold the left over leaving two inches away from the right.

4. Do that again.

Splendid.

TRILLIUM *

It is simple, but grand.

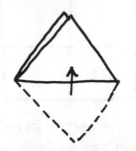

1. Fold the bottom up to form a trinagle.

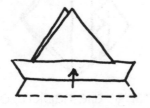

2. Fold the bottom up one-fourth of the distance.

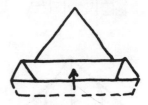

3. Fold it again, the same distance.

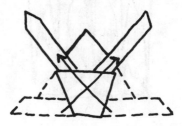

4. Now, crisscross the ends, lay it on a plate with either side up.

LEIGHA

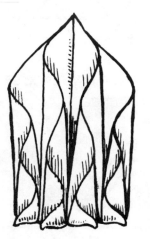

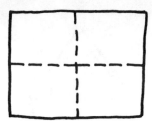

1. Fold the napkin in half and in half again.

2. Arrange the napkin so that all loose points are to the right.

Fold back the first layer — all the way to the left. Accordion fold it.

3. Fold back the second layer and accordion fold it so that the accordion fold is lying next to, and touching the first layer.

4. Fold back the third layer and accordion fold it so that the accordion fold is lying next to, and touching the second layer.

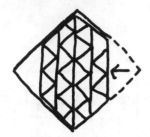

5. Accordion fold the fourth layer so that it is lying next to and touching the third layer.

7. Fold the top tip and the bottom tip underneath.

6. Fold the left side triangle underneath.

If you have something else to fall back on, that's what you might do . . . fall back.

DIAMONDS*

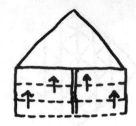

This looks dynamite with a printed napkin.

1. Put your napkin flat on the table and fold it exactly in three parts.

2. End view.

3. Fold both the left and right corners down along the dotted line shown.

   Flip over left to right, smooth side up.

4. Turn up the bottom edges by making two equal folds, following the dotted lines.

   Holding the bottom edges in place, flip over left to right.

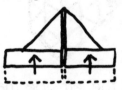

5. Fold the bottom, double folded edges up. See diagram.

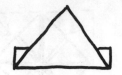

6. Flip over left to right.

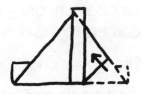

7. Take the bottom right corner and fold up to the center.

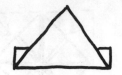

8. Do likewise with the left side.

You may present this fold using either side.

In order to do things people can't, you've got to do things people won't.

TURN FLAT INTO FLUFFY*

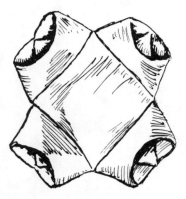

The uses are similar to the Artichoke. Make sure you are using a "full bodied" napkin.

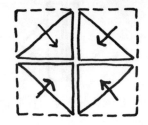

1. Lay napkin flat and bring all four corners to the center.
Flip over left to right.

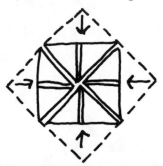

2. Again fold all corners to the center and form another square.
Flip over left to right.

3. Once again, bring all four corners to the center.

Flip it over once more.

And magic, the four corners pop out, and you are ready for your special presentation.

MISCELLANEOUS INDEX

*A napkin printed only on one side may be used.

An Idea:
Use a large napkin that complements your table linens and wrap it around a flower pot. Tie with a ribbon and use it as a centerpiece.

WHY KNOT?*

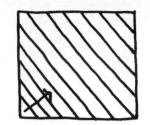

1. Roll the square napkin starting at one corner.

2. Now tie a knot in the center.

   Place this around a plate or directly on a plate.

Your dinner folding will not be complete unless you fold individual . . .

OSHIBORIS

Begin with a square terry wash cloth.

1. Fold the cloth in thirds.

2. The end view.

3. Roll the terry cloth to the end.

4. With the outside edge free, hold the inside and turn it inside out, so it's contained.
Roll enough for the guests and place them in a pan, moisten thoroughly with water.

*Fragrant the water with your favorite cologne.

*Or add lemon juice to cut the grease.

Now place in an oven, 250 degrees F. till thoroughly warm, or zap in your microwave.

POMPOUS PEACOCK *

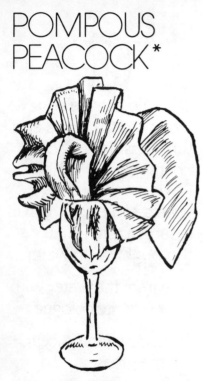

This one is somewhat impractical because it requires two napkins, but it makes a fun centerpiece.

The first half is Marnie's Mockingbird on page 50.

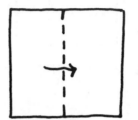

1. Now, take a second napkin and fold it in half.

2. Accordion fold the napkin all the way down.

3. Fold the napkin in half

4. and place in a wine glass over the first fold, fan out pleats to resemble wings.

THAT WAS A
GOOD YEAR . . . .

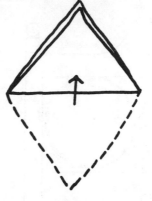

1. Flip the bottom up to form a triangle.

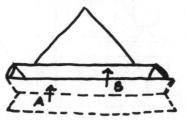

2A. Next, fold a hem along the folded edge, about two inches wide.

B. Repeat step 2A, and fold again.

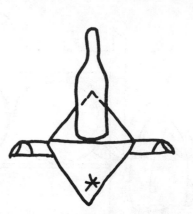

3. With the napkin on a flat surface, * pull back the top layer.

Set a bottle on the napkin, bring all four points up around the bottle and tie the "handles" into a knot.

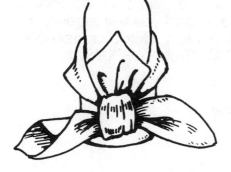

This adds that extra touch to a fine bottle of wine.

Dear Fellow Frumpy Fold Fan,

If you know of a napkin fold that I do not already have included in this book, I would like to hear from you.

If you send me the fold with enough directions so that I may learn how to fold your fold, and it gets included in the next edition, your personal name will appear on that page and you will receive a complimentary, autographed copy of OLGA'S FRUMPY FOLDS.

With Warm Wishes,

Olga

Send me your name, address and the free directions to:

SCHPITFEIR ENTERPRISES
P.O. Box 1426
Minnetonka, MN 55343